The Minneapolis General Math Project

CHARTING YOUR COURSE

Map Skills

CHADWICK LIBRARY
Iowa Wesleyan College
MT. PLEASANT, IOWA 52641

DALE
SEYMOUR
PUBLICATIONS
P.O. BOX 10888
PALO ALTO, CA 94303

The Minneapolis General Math Project was developed by
the Minneapolis Public Schools, Minneapolis, Minnesota.

Project Co-Directors: Pamela Katzman
Jackie McClees

Production and Artwork: Ingrid Holley

Project Team: Cheri Carlson
Paul Dillenberger
Al Hoogheem
Mike Hughes
Mary Indelicato
Bill Robbins
Marion Thorne
Les Twedell

Contributors: Anne Bartel
Carol Borne
Vicki DeVoss
Ron Fish
John Hendrickson
Barb Kitlinski
John Maus
Debii (Winberg) Nelson

**Mathematics Consultant,
Minneapolis Public Schools:** Ross Taylor

The Project Team wishes to thank those teachers and students
in the Minneapolis Public School System who field-tested and
evaluated these materials as they were being developed.

Copyright © 1983 by Dale Seymour Publications. All rights reserved. Printed in the
United States of America. Published simultaneously in Canada.

Limited Reproduction Permission: The publisher grants permission to
reproduce up to 100 copies of any part of this book for noncommercial classroom
or individual use. Any further duplication is prohibited.

ISBN 0-86651-119-9

Order Number DS01393

bcdefghi-MA-876

DALE
SEYMOUR
PUBLICATIONS
P.O. BOX 10888
PALO ALTO, CA 94303

CONTENTS

The Minneapolis General Math Project   iv

Contents of the Project   vi

Contents of CHARTING YOUR COURSE   viii

The Lessons   1

Come to Grips with Graphs

Road Distances

Travel Tips

Day Finder

Is It Your Day?

NOV 2 1 1991

THE MINNEAPOLIS GENERAL
MATH PROJECT

What is the Minneapolis General Math Project?

The Minneapolis General Math project consists of 8 different books containing a total of 61 teaching units. The teaching units were developed to supplement the teaching of basic mathematical skills as identified by the National Council of Supervisors of Mathematics (NCSM). The lessons in each unit reinforce the use of basic math skills while exploring topics which interest secondary school students.

Each of the books in the Minneapolis General Math Project corresponds to one or more basic skill areas.

BOOK	BASIC SKILLS
In a Word . . . Checking Out Patterns	Problem Solving
The Whole of It Part and Parcel Watch Your Wallet	Applying Mathematics to Everyday Situations Appropriate Computational Skills
A Reasonably Close Encounter	Alertness to Reasonableness of Results Estimation and Approximation
The Size of It	Geometry Measurement
Charting Your Course	Reading, Interpreting Constructing Tables Charts, and Graphs

Two basic skill areas identified by the NCSM, Using Mathematics to Predict and Computer Literacy, are *not* reinforced in the books. There are other materials available that thoroughly cover these skills.

Who can use the Minneapolis General Math Project?

The lessons in the Minneapolis General Math Project were designed for ninth-grade general mathematics courses. They are appropriate for use in any secondary school situation where reinforcing the use of basic math skills is desired. The lessons also can be used with adults who are earning high school equivalency certificates.

What do the books contain?

Each book contains from 4 to 11 units. A unit consists of blackline master lesson pages which focus on a particular topic of interest such as earthquakes, maps, tipping, or palindromes. There is a teacher's page describing the contents of the unit and giving suggestions for its use. Some units include a test. An answer key (which includes answers for test items) is provided for each unit.

How can the books be used?

The units of the Minneapolis General Math Project can be used independently of one another for individual, group, or full-class activities, depending on your classroom organization and needs. You may select the units you wish to use and teach them in different orders. In some cases, a particular order of presentation is recommended.

The books are designed so the pages can be easily removed and reproduced by Thermofax, Xerox, or a similar process. You can make either transparencies for overhead projection or pages for student use.

The lessons within a unit are sequential. Most teachers copy all the lesson pages for a given unit at once and provide one set for each student to be used as consumable workbooks. You can make the units non-consumable by creating a blank answer sheet for your students. However, any puzzles should be reproduced for individual student use.

CONTENTS OF THE PROJECT

The following chart shows the books and units for the complete Minneapolis General Math Project. All units reinforce the use of whole numbers. Some units also reinforce the use of fractions, decimals, percent, or signed numbers.

	WHOLE NOS.	FRACTIONS	DECIMALS	PERCENT	SIGNED NOS.
IN A WORD . . .					
Operation: Word Problem	✔		✔		
De-Vine Word Problems	✔		✔		
Read & Reason	✔		✔		
Calculators with a Twist	✔		✔		
CHECKING OUT PATTERNS					
Simple Sequences	✔				
Sequences	✔	✔			
Fibonacci Sequence	✔				
Fibonacci Fractions	✔	✔	✔		
Picture This	✔				
We The Jury	✔		✔		
Easy Does It	✔				
Fanciful Formulas	✔	✔			
THE WHOLE OF IT					
Mom, Dad, Bob & Lil	✔				
The Key to Locks	✔				
Telephone Trivia	✔				
License Plates	✔				
MPG	✔				
Calorie Countdown	✔				
Calories Count Up	✔				
Earthquakes	✔				
PART AND PARCEL					
Buttonholes	✔	✔			
A Fishy Tale	✔	✔			
Stock Up	✔	✔			
Pizza for Breakfast	✔	✔			
The Fraction Link	✔	✔			
Right Off the Bat	✔	✔	✔		
Hannah, Anna, Otto & Ada	✔		✔		
Carat with a "C"	✔		✔		
Karat with a "K"	✔	✔		✔	
Bionic Betty	✔			✔	
Tipping	✔			✔	

	WHOLE NOS.	FRACTIONS	DECIMALS	PERCENT	SIGNED NOS.
WATCH YOUR WALLET					
You Can Bank On It	✓				
Money Matters	✓				
Sales Tax	✓				
Wise Buys	✓				
A REASONABLY CLOSE ENCOUNTER					
About "About"	✓				
Making Some Headway	✓				
Making an Adjustment	✓				
Just Around the Corner	✓		✓		
Be Reasonable	✓		✓		
Divide and Conquer	✓				
Everyday Estimation	✓		✓		
Making You Percentable	✓	✓	✓	✓	
Fraction Action	✓	✓			
The Money Round-Up	✓		✓		
THE SIZE OF IT					
Getting Around	✓				
Horsing Around	✓		✓		
Cover Up	✓				
State of Bedlam	✓		✓		
Maximum's Area	✓				
Perimeter Is Your Area	✓		✓		
Pizza Pi	✓		✓		
Pan Plan	✓		✓		
Temperature	✓				
The Weather Report	✓				✓
Is It On the Level?	✓				✓
CHARTING YOUR COURSE					
Come to Grips with Graphs	✓	✓	✓	✓	
Road Distances	✓				
Travel Tips	✓	✓	✓		
Day Finder	✓				
Is It Your Day?	✓				

CONTENTS OF *CHARTING YOUR COURSE*

UNIT	DESCRIPTION
Come to Grips with Graphs	Presents a variety of graphs to read and interpret. Uses whole numbers, easy fractions, and easy percents.
Road Distances	Presents mileage charts to read and interpret. Uses whole numbers.
Travel Tips	Presents maps on which distances must be estimated. Uses whole numbers and simple fractions.
Day Finder	Presents a formula for determining the day given a date. (Use of this formula requires reading charts.) Uses addition and division of whole numbers.
Is It Your Day?	Presents the Biorhythm Theory and then uses biorhythm cycle graphs to find various biorhythms. Uses whole number addition, multiplication, and division.

general math project

minneapolis public schools

UNIT: COME TO GRIPS WITH GRAPHS

DESCRIPTION: Samples of pictographs, bar graphs, line graphs and circle graphs are given in this unit with suggestions as to how to read them. Students are then asked to read and answer questions on additional graphs.

SKILLS TO BE REINFORCED: reading graphs

PREREQUISITE SKILLS: working with whole numbers

percent of a number

fraction of a number ($\frac{1}{2}$, $\frac{1}{4}$, $\frac{3}{4}$)

LENGTH: 16 pages; 3-5 days

TEACHER NOTES: You may choose to have students make some additional graphs of their own, even though this unit does not deal with making graphs.

This unit is divided into several sections: Pictographs, Bar Graphs, Line Graphs and Circle Graphs. You may want to do this unit by sections if the whole unit would be overwhelming for your students.

NO TEST: You could use the puzzles from this unit as tests.

© 1983 by Dale Seymour Publications

Come to grips with GRAPHS

* Read these facts:

The population of the United States has increased ten times since 1850. In 1850 there were 23 million people in the U.S. By 1900 there were 76 million people. When the census was taken in 1950, there were about 150 million people in the U.S. Although the figures are not complete for 1980, it is estimated that there are about 230 million people presently living in the U.S.

* Here are the same facts shown on a bar graph

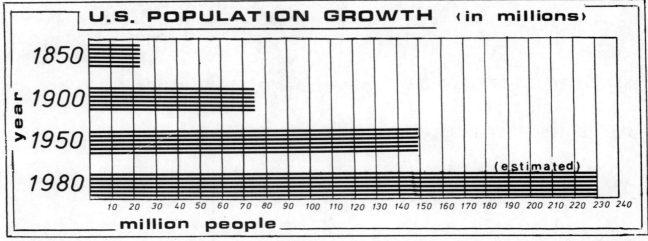

Use either the paragraph above or the graph to answer these questions.

1. In what year mentioned above were the the FEWEST people living in the U.S.? _____
    (1)

2. In what year mentioned were the MOST people living in the U.S.? _____
    (2)

3. About how many people were living in the U.S. in 1950? _____
    (3)

4. There were about 76 million people in the U.S. in _____?
    (4)

* Which did you find the easier to use when you answered the questions, the facts written out in words or the graph? _____
(5)

> In this unit you will use several kinds of graphs: PICTOGRAPHS, BAR GRAPHS, LINE GRAPHS AND CIRCLE GRAPHS.
>
> Graphs show facts which could be written out in words but which are easier to "see" than to read.

© 1983 by Dale Seymour Publications

PICTOGRAPHS are used to compare information.

Pictographs are graphs which use a picture symbol to represent a **certain number of objects.**

TO READ A PICTOGRAPH

1. Read the title of the graph.
   This will tell you the topic of the graph.

2. Read the "key". This will tell you
   "how many" each symbol stands for.

3. Now read and compare the information
   shown on the graph.

Capacity of Football Stadiums

Kingdome	🏟🏟🏟🏟🏟🏟🏟
Superdome	🏟🏟🏟🏟🏟🏟🏟🏟
Texas Stadium	🏟🏟🏟🏟🏟🏟
Pontiac Stadium	🏟🏟🏟🏟🏟🏟🏟🏟
Metrodome	🏟🏟🏟🏟🏟🏟🏟
Tampa Stadium	🏟🏟🏟🏟🏟🏟🏟

KEY
🏟
10,000 people

1. What is the title of this pictograph? _____
   (6)

2. What does each symbol 🏟 stand for? _____
   (7)

3. Which stadium can hold the most people? _____
   (8)

4. Which stadium holds the fewest people? _____
   (9)

5. To find out about how many people a given stadium can hold, add 10,000 for
   each 🏟 shown next to its name.
   Tampa Stadium can hold about how many people? _____
   (10)

6. The symbol 🏟 stands for $\frac{1}{2}$ as many as 🏟.   Since 🏟 stands for 10,000
   people, 🏟 stands for _____ people.
   (11)

7. Which stadium can hold about 75,000 people? _____
   (12)

8. How many people can attend a game at the Metrodome in Minneapolis?

   _____
   (13)

© 1983 by Dale Seymour Publications   Come to Grips with Graphs   2

Estimated Gas Mileage *

Chevette	
Chevy Malibu	
Datsun B210	
Dodge Diplomat	
Ford Fiesta	
Pontiac Catalina	

KEY: = 5 mpg   mpg means miles per gallon   ★ **1978** Highway Driving

According to this graph...

1. What is the title of this pictograph? _____ (14)

2. What does each symbol stand for? _____ (15)

3. What does each ½ symbol stand for? _____ (16)

4. Which car can be driven the farthest on a gallon of gas? _____ (17)

5. Which car goes the fewest miles on a gallon of gas? _____ (18)

6. Which car gets about 35 mpg? _____ (19)

7. About how many mpg does a Chevy Malibu get? _____ (20)

8. What is the gas mileage for a Pontiac Catalina? _____ (21)

9. A VW Rabbit gets about 35 mpg. How many symbols should be used to represent this mpg?

_____ (22)

10. Add a VW Rabbit and its mileage symbols to the chart.

(23)

© 1983 by Dale Seymour Publications

CANINE COUNT

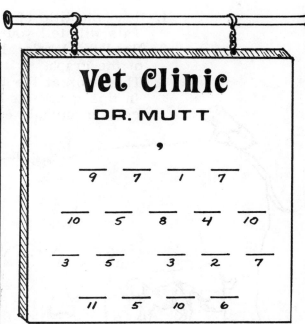

To find out **Dr. Mutt's** motto, work each problem below. Find the answer in the Code Box and put the corresponding letter above the problem number in the message. A problem number may appear more than once in the message.

AMERICAN KENNEL CLUB REGISTRATIONS IN 1978

Poodles

Doberman Pinschers

German Shepherds

Irish Setters

Shetland Sheepdog

Siberian Huskies

Chihuahuas

Boston Terriers

Weimaraners

= 10,000

Vet Clinic
DR. MUTT

,

___ ___ ___ ___
9   7   1   7

___ ___ ___ ___ ___
10   5   8   4   10

___ ___ ___ ___ ___
3   5   3   2   7

___ ___ ___ ___
11   5   10   6

1. About how many German Shepherds were registered in 1978? _____

2. About how many more Dobermans were registered than Boston Terriers? _____

3. About how many Weimaraners were registered? _____

4. About how many Shetland Sheepdogs were registered? _____

5. There were about _____ Boston Terriers registered.

6. There were about _____ Poodles registered.

7. About how many more Irish Setters were registered than Chihuahuas? _____

8. What is the total number of Weimaraners and Shetland Sheepdogs registered? _____

9. The toy breeds would have $10\frac{1}{2}$ symbols. About how many dogs does that represent? _____

10. The Silky Terrier would have $\frac{1}{4}$ of a symbol. About how many dogs does that represent? _____

11. The Alaskan Malamute would have 3/4 of a symbol. About how many dogs does that represent? _____

Code Box

2500	G
5000	T
7500	D
10,000	O
15,000	E
25,000	N
30,000	I
60,000	R
70,000	H
100,000	S
105,000	W

© 1983 by Dale Seymour Publications

BAR GRAPHS

show "how many" with thick bars of different lengths.

Bar Graphs are used to <u>compare</u> information or amounts.

TO READ A BAR GRAPH

1. Read the title of the bar graph.
   This will tell you the topic of the graph.
2. Read the labels along the side and bottom of the graph.
3. Then look at the BARS (the dark lines).
   In this graph the lengths of the bars tell how many years certain animals can be expected to live.

1. What is the title of this graph?

   _____

   _____ (24)

2. The numbers on the side of the graph stand for

   _____ (25)

3. About how long can a whale be expected to live?

   _____ (26)

4. Which can be expected to live longer, a baboon or a buffalo?

   _____ (27)

5. Which animal mentioned on this graph has the longest lifespan?

   _____ (28)

   the shortest?

   _____ (29)

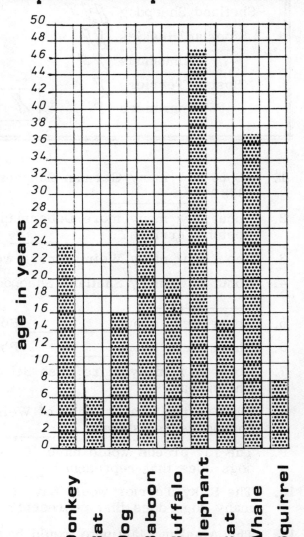

Expected Lifespan of Animals

age in years: Donkey, Bat, Dog, Baboon, Buffalo, Elephant, Cat, Whale, Squirrel

© 1983 by Dale Seymour Publications

Arrests in Minnesota · 1975

Not all crimes for which there were arrests are listed on this graph.

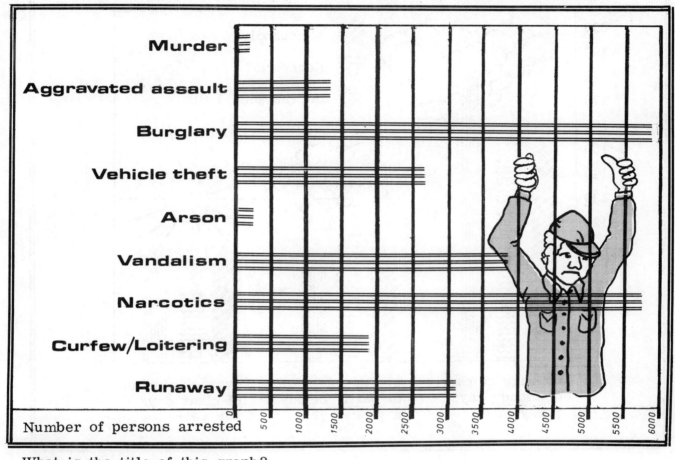

Number of persons arrested

1. What is the title of this graph? _____
    (30)

2. What do the numbers along the bottom of the graph represent? _____

    _____
    (31)

3. Are all the arrests made in Minnesota included on this bar graph? _____
    (32)

4. About how many people were arrested for: vehicle theft _____
    vandalism _____ ; being a runaway _____ ?
    (34)   (35)   (33)

5. For what crime listed on the graph were the most arrests made? _____
    (36)
    the fewest arrests made? _____
    (37)

6. In 1975, 19,500 people were arrested for larceny.

    Why couldn't larceny be included on this graph? _____

    _____
    (38)

7. For which crime were there about 1300 arrests in 1975? _____
    (39)

© 1983 by Dale Seymour Publications

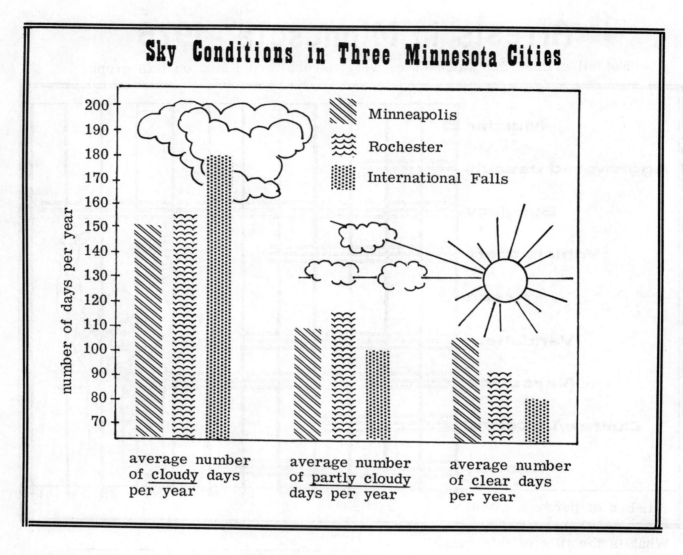

Sky Conditions in Three Minnesota Cities

Legend:
- Minneapolis
- Rochester
- International Falls

y-axis: number of days per year (70 to 200)

average number of <u>cloudy</u> days per year

average number of <u>partly cloudy</u> days per year

average number of <u>clear</u> days per year

1. What is the title of this graph? _____
   (40)

2. What do the numbers on the side of the graph represent? _____
   _____
   (41)

3. What three Minnesota cities are being compared in this graph?
   _____ _____ _____
   (42)

4. Which city of the three has the most clear days? _____
   (43)
   about how many? _____
   (44)

5. Which city has the most cloudy days? _____ about how
   (45)
   many? _____
   (46)

6. Which city has the most partly cloudy days? _____
   (47)
   about how many? _____
   (48)

© 1983 by Dale Seymour Publications

BAR EXAM

What is a statistician who examines graphs called?

$\overline{3}$ $\overline{10}$ $\overline{5}$ $\overline{2}$ $\overline{4}$ $\overline{8}$ $\overline{1}$ $\overline{9}$ $\overline{6}$ $\overline{7}$

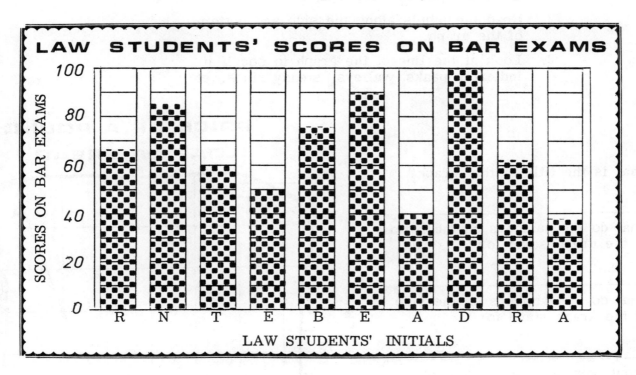

For each problem below, find the correct bar. Put the initial at the bottom of that bar above the problem number in the message.

1. This student got 85 correct.

2. This student received a score of 62.

3. This poor student only got 40 correct.

4. This student got 40 <u>wrong.</u>

5. This student received the lowest score.

6. This student got 30 more correct than the person with the lowest score.

7. This unlikely lawyer got only half the problems correct.

8. This student got 1/10 of the problems wrong.

9. This student got 100% correct.

10. This student got three-fourths of the test correct.

© 1983 by Dale Seymour Publications

A # LINE GRAPH is a graph on which points are

connected by a line to show change over a period of time. Predictions about future trends can often be made by looking at a line graph.

TO READ A LINE GRAPH

1. Read the title of the graph. This will tell you the topic of the graph.

2. Read the labels along the side and bottom of the graph.

3. Look at the line of the graph to see if it indicates peaks, valleys, steady rises, etc.

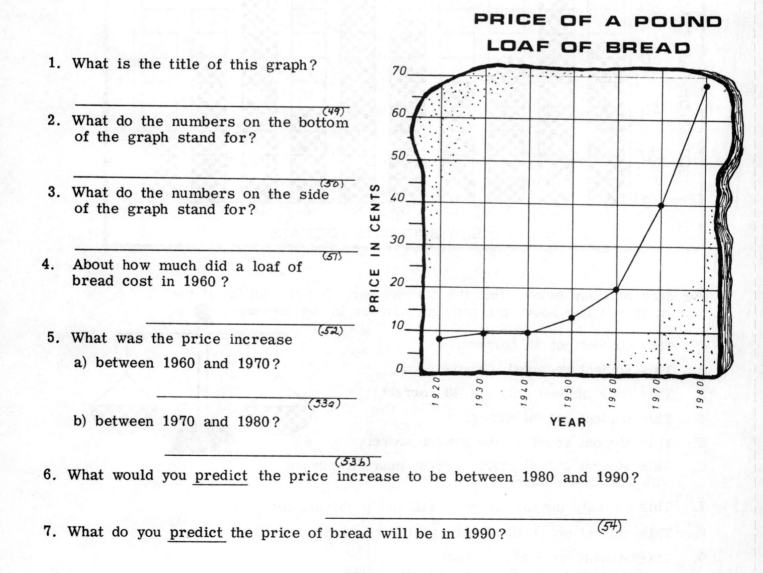

PRICE OF A POUND
LOAF OF BREAD

1. What is the title of this graph?

_____ (49)

2. What do the numbers on the bottom of the graph stand for?

_____ (50)

3. What do the numbers on the side of the graph stand for?

_____ (51)

4. About how much did a loaf of bread cost in 1960 ?

_____ (52)

5. What was the price increase

a) between 1960 and 1970 ?

_____ (53a)

b) between 1970 and 1980 ?

_____ (53b)

6. What would you <u>predict</u> the price increase to be between 1980 and 1990 ?

_____ (54)

7. What do you <u>predict</u> the price of bread will be in 1990 ?

_____ (55)

© 1983 by Dale Seymour Publications

Winter Olympics

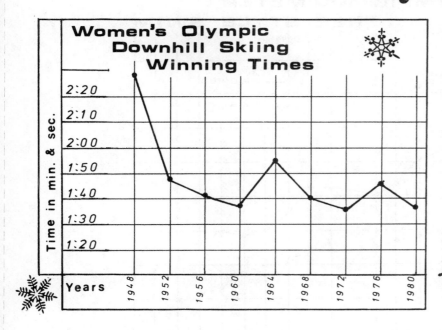

1. This graph shows what kind of information?

   _____

   _____
   (56)

2. In what <u>years</u> was the winning time close to 1:40?

   _____
   (57)

3. Estimate the winning time

   in 1964 _____
   (58)

   in 1980 _____
   (59)

1. This line graph shows winning times for which event?

   _____
   (60)

2. In what year did a woman win in about 45 seconds?

   _____
   (61)

3. About what was the winning time for men in 1976?

   _____
   (62)

4. About how far apart were the men's and women's winning times in 1980?

   _____
   (63)

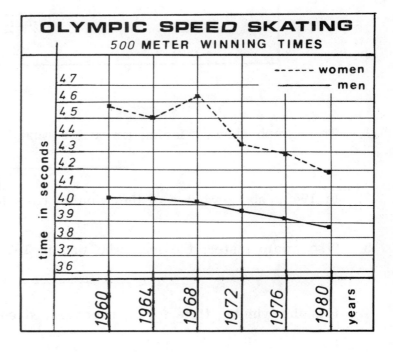

5. What would you predict as the winning time in 1984 ...

   for women _____   for men _____
   (64)   (65)

6. Do you think that the women's winning time will equal the men's in the next four Olympics? _____ why or why not? _____
   (66)

   _____
   (67)

© 1983 by Dale Seymour Publications   Come to Grips with Graphs   10

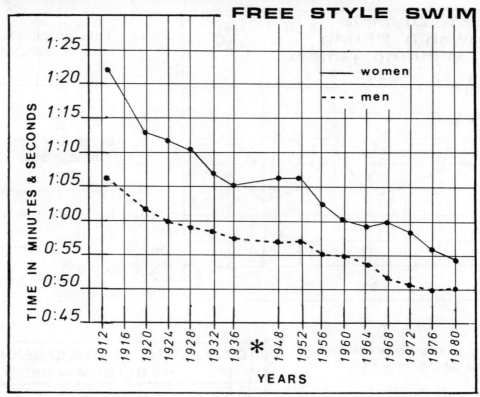

SUMMER OLYMPIC 100 METER FREE STYLE SWIM

——— women

- - - - men

TIME IN MINUTES & SECONDS

YEARS

✳ Interrupted by W. W. II

1. This graph shows winning times for what Olympic event?

    _____
    (68)

2. In 1948, about what was the winning time for women?

    _____
    (69)

3. Who swam faster: the man who won in 1920 or the woman who won in 1976?

    _____
    (70)

4. Has the winning time for men decreased each year?

    _____
    (71)

5. By how much did the winning time for women decrease from 1912 to 1976?

    _____
    (72)

6. What would you predict as the winning time for this event in the next summer Olympics?

    for women _____ for men _____
    (73)   (74)

© 1983 by Dale Seymour Publications

WHAT'S THE ANGLE?

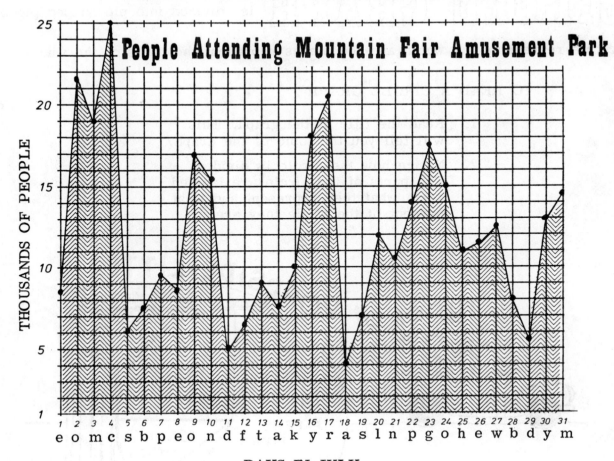

People Attending Mountain Fair Amusement Park

THOUSANDS OF PEOPLE

DAYS IN JULY

Find the answer to each problem using the line graph. At the bottom of each day is a letter. Put the letter above the problem number in the message.

1. On what day did the most people go to the park?

2. On what day did the fewest people go to the park?

3. When did the same number of people go to the park as on July 6?

4. On what day did 20,500 people attend?

5. On what day did 9000 people attend?

6. On what day did 17,500 people attend?

7. 8500 people attended the park on which day?

8. On what day did 12,000 people attend?

9. On what day did 11,500 people go to the park?

10. On what day did 15,500 people go to the park?

What do you call a broken angle?

$\overline{}_{3}\quad \overline{}_{4}\ \overline{}_{9}\ \overline{}_{1}\ \overline{}_{5}\ \overline{}_{2}\ \overline{}_{10}\ \overline{}_{6}\ \overline{}_{8}\ \overline{}_{7}$

© 1983 by Dale Seymour Publications

A CIRCLE GRAPH is divided into pie shaped pieces.

The circle represents the whole and the pieces represent the parts of the whole.

TO READ A CIRCLE GRAPH

1. Read the title of the graph. This will tell you the topic of the graph.

2. Notice how the circle is divided. The parts of the circle are labeled as to what they represent and what percent of the whole they are.

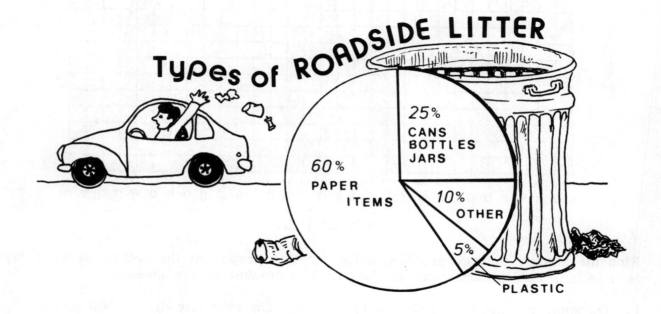

Types of ROADSIDE LITTER

25% CANS BOTTLES JARS

60% PAPER ITEMS

10% OTHER

5%

PLASTIC

1. What is the title of this circle graph? _____
    (75)

2. What percent of roadside litter is paper? _____
    (76)

3. What percent of roadside litter is cans, jars and bottles? _____
    (77)

4. What waste makes up about 5% of the litter? _____
    (78)

5. 10% of the litter is titled "OTHER". What might be some items in this category?
    _____
    (79)

© 1983 by Dale Seymour Publications

HOW FAMILY INCOME*IS SPENT

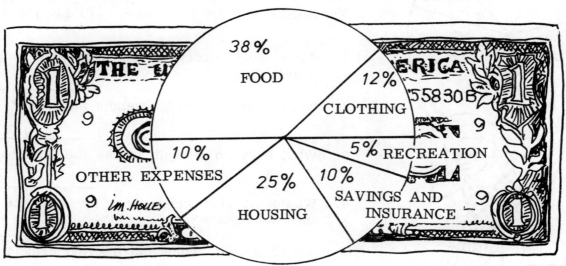

38% FOOD

12% CLOTHING

5% RECREATION

10% OTHER EXPENSES

25% HOUSING

10% SAVINGS AND INSURANCE

net income

1. What is the largest expense of an average family? _____ (80)

2. About 25% of a family's income goes for what? _____ (81)

3. The money a person would use to go roller skating would fall into what category? _____ (82)

   How much of the income would fall into this category? _____ (83)

4. A family brings home $1000 a month. According to this graph, about how much would this family spend each month on clothes? _____ (84)

   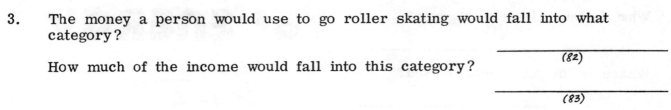

   12% of 1000 is .12 × 1000 =

5. A family brings home $500 a month. According to this graph, about how much would this family spend monthly on housing?

   25% of 500 is ____ × 500 = _____ (85)

6. A family brings home $750 a month. According to this graph, about how much would this family spend on food each month? _____ (86)

© 1983 by Dale Seymour Publications

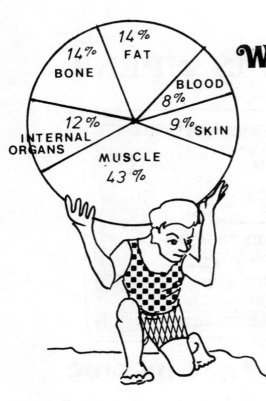

Weights of Body Components*

✳ BASED ON AN AVERAGE 170 LB. MALE

1. About what percent of the total body weight is bone?

   _____
   (87)

2. What body component weighs the most?

   _____
   (88)

3. What body component weighs the least?

   _____
   (89)

4. Would the skin weigh more or less than the internal organs?

   _____
   (90)

5. Would the fat, bone and internal organs weigh more or less than the muscle?

   _____
   (91)

USERS of ENERGY

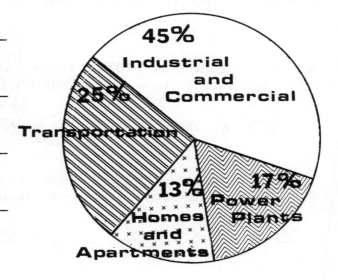

1. What is the title of this graph?

   _____
   (92)

2. Where is the most energy used?

   _____
   (93)

   How much of the total is this?

   _____
   (94)

3. Where is the least energy used?

   _____
   (95)

   How much of the total is this?

   _____
   (96)

4. How is 25% of the energy used?

   _____
   (97)

5. Electrical power plants have to use energy to make electricity. What percent of the total energy do they use?

   _____
   (98)

© 1983 by Dale Seymour Publications

I'll buy that!

To find out what this doodle is, answer each question below. Then find the answer in the Code Box and put the corresponding letter above the problem number. A problem number may appear more than once in the message.

$\overline{11}$ $\overline{8}$ $\overline{1}$ $\overline{4}$ $\overline{9}$ $\overline{3}$ $\overline{7}$ $\overline{5}$

and

$\overline{10}$ $\overline{6}$ $\overline{2}$ $\overline{9}$

DIVISION OF FOOD DOLLAR

sugars 15%

fruits & vegetables 21%

flour products 12%

milk products 14%

meats 38%

1. What percent of a dollar is spent on sugars? _____
2. What percent is spent on milk products? _____
3. How much more of the food dollar is spent on meats than on milk products? _____
4. If you add all the percentages in the circle graph, what do you get? _____
5. Does the average person spend more of the food dollar on milk products, fruits and vegetables than on meat? s? _____
6. What percent is spent on meats and flour products? _____
7. Is more spent on meats that on sugars and flour products? _____
8. According to the graph, if you spend $1.00 for food, $.38 of it will be spent for meat. If you spend $10.00 for food, how much of it will you spend for meat? _____
9. If you spend $5.00 for food, how much of it will you spend for milk products? _____
10. If you spend $20.00 for food, how much of it will you spend for fruits & vegetables and flour products? _____
11. If you spend $6.00 for food, how much of it will you spend for sugar products? _____

CODE BOX

14%	L
15%	A
24%	E
50%	I
100%	C
YES	R
NO	S
$.70	K
$.90	Q
$3.80	U
$6.60	M

Hint:
14% of 5.00
.14 × 5.00 = _____

© 1983 by Dale Seymour Publications

1. 1850
2. 1980
3. 150 million
4. 1900
5. graph
6. Capacity of Football Stadiums
7. 10,000 people
8. Pontiac Stadium
9. Texas Stadium
10. 70,000
11. 5000
12. Superdome
13. 65,000
14. Estimated Gas Mileage
15. 5 mpg
16. $2\frac{1}{2}$ mpg
17. Ford Fiesta
18. Dodge Diplomat
19. Chevette
20. 25 mpg
21. $22\frac{1}{2}$ mpg
22. 7 symbols
23. (add VW Rabbit and 7 symbols)
24. Expected Lifespan of Animals
25. age in years

26. 37 years
27. baboon
28. elephant
29. bat
30. Arrests in Minnesota · 1975
31. number of persons arrested
32. no
33. about 2700
34. about 3800
35. about 3100
36. Burglary
37. Murder
38. the graph is not long enough
39. Aggravated Assault
40. Sky Conditions in Three Minnesota Cities
41. number of days per year for each condition
42. Minneapolis, Rochester, International Falls
43. Minneapolis
44. 105
45. International Falls
46. 180
47. Rochester
48. 115
49. Price of a Pound Loaf of Bread
50. year

© 1983 by Dale Seymour Publications

51. price in cents
52. 20¢
53. a) 20¢ b) 28¢
54. around 40¢
55. around $1.10
56. Women's Olympic Downhill Skiing Winning Times
57. 1956 and 1968
58. about 1:55
59. about
60. Olympic Speed Skating
61. 1964
62. 39 seconds
63. about 3 seconds
64. 40-41 seconds
65. 37-38 seconds
66. no (some may say yes)
67. answers will vary
68. Summer Olympic 100 Meter Free Style Swim
69. 1:06
70. the woman in 1976
71. no
72. about 26 seconds
73. about 54 seconds
74. about 49 seconds
75. Types of Roadside Litter

76. 60%
77. 25%
78. plastic
79. food, tires, metal, etc.
80. food
81. housing
82. recreation
83. 5%
84. $120
85. $125
86. $285
87. 14%
88. muscle
89. blood
90. less
91. less
92. Users of Energy
93. Industrial and Commercial
94. 45%
95. Homes and Apartments
96. 13%
97. Transportation
98. 17%

© 1983 by Dale Seymour Publications

PUZZLE ANSWERS

page 4 (Message Puzzle):
WE'RE GOING TO THE DOGS

page 8 (Message puzzle):
A BARTENDER

page 12 (Message Puzzle):
A RECTANGLE

page 16 (Message Puzzle):
QUACKERS AND MILK

general math project

minneapolis public schools

UNIT: ROAD DISTANCES

DESCRIPTION: In this unit, students first learn to use distance charts
like the ones on maps to find distances between two
given towns. Then they find total distances from one
town to another with towns between. The charts are
also used to find round trip distances and to locate the
town closest to a given town.

SKILLS TO BE REINFORCED: reading a chart with two scales; whole number
addition

PREREQUISITE SKILLS: none

LENGTH: 9 pages; two or three days

TEST ANSWERS:

1. 2869

2. Los Angeles

3. Omaha, NE; 867

4. 1361; 663; 2024

5. 169

6. 28

7. 278

8. St. Paul

© 1983 by Dale Seymour Publications

Road Distances

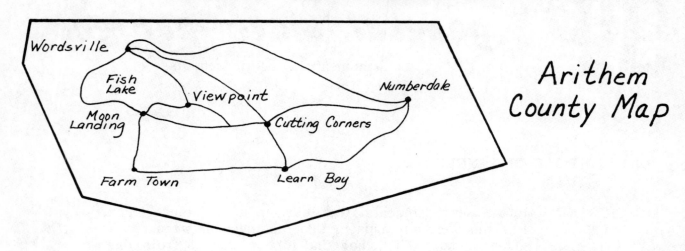

Arithem County Map

Distances between towns on a map can often be found by looking at a chart like this:

DISTANCES FOR ARITHEM COUNTY distances in kilometers (km)	Cutting Corners	Farm Town	Learn Bay	Moon Landing	Numberdale	Viewpoint	Wordsville
Cutting Corners		62	30	56	43	45	40
Farm Town	62		75	28	106	54	76
Learn Bay	30	75		88	39	77	72
Moon Landing	56	28	88		101	25	47
Numberdale	43	106	39	101		90	68
Viewpoint	45	54	77	25	90		30
Wordsville	40	76	72	47	68	30	

What is the title of the chart? _____

_____ (1)

The numbers in the chart represent distances between towns. These numbers do not stand for miles, they stand for _____ (2)

© 1983 by Dale Seymour Publications

Look at the chart for Arithem County on page 1.

To find the distance from one city to another city (from Numberdale to Viewpoint, for example), follow these steps:

1 Find "the first" city (Numberdale) on the side of the chart.

2 Find "the other" city (Viewpoint) at the top of the chart.

3 Move your fingers across and down until your fingers meet. Numberdale and Viewpoint are 90 km apart.

1 Now, use steps 1, 2, and 3 to find the distance from Farm Town to Learn Bay. _____ km.
(3)

2 From Cutting Corners to Viewpoint is _____ kilometers.
(4)

3 How far is it from Learn Bay to Numberdale? _____ km.
(5)

4 How many kilometers is it from Farm Town to Numberdale? _____ km.
(6)

5 To go from Wordsville to Moon Landing with a stopover at Viewpoint, you will have to add two distances together.

First, find the distance from Wordsville to Viewpoint _____ km
(7)

Now, find the distance from Viewpoint to Moon Landing _____ km
(8)

add these

What is the total distance of this trip? _____ km
(9)

6 Find the distance from Numberdale to Cutting Corners with a stopover in Learn Bay.

Numberdale to Learn Bay _____ km
(10)

Learn Bay to Cutting Corners _____ km
(11)

Total trip _____ km
(12)

7 According to the chart, it is 43 kilometers to go directly from Numberdale to Cutting Corners. How many extra kilometers does a stopover at Learn Bay add to the trip? _____ km
(13)

See problem 6

© 1983 by Dale Seymour Publications

U.S. ROAD DISTANCES (kilometers)	Austin, TX	Baltimore, MD	Birmingham, AL	Chicago, IL	Denver, CO	Jackson, MS	Little Rock, AR	Los Angeles, CA	Mpls-St. Paul, MN	New York, NY	Omaha, NE	San Francisco, CA
Austin, TX		2529	1257	1823	1459	861	795	2227	1955	2843	1397	2869
Baltimore, MD	2529		1273	1102	2624	1670	1752	4262	1754	301	1870	4626
Birmingham, AL	1257	1273		1051	2095	397	632	3319	2102	1574	1475	3847
Chicago, IL	1823	1102	1051		1630	1212	1046	3366	663	1353	763	3519
Denver, CO	1459	2624	2095	1630		1923	1553	1862	1361	3002	867	2034
Jackson, MS	861	1670	397	1212	1923		418	2922	1691	1971	1397	3498
Little Rock, AR	795	1752	632	1046	1553	418		2727	1334	2048	978	3255
Los Angeles, CA	2227	4262	3319	3366	1862	2922	2727		3125	4500	2685	652
Mpls-St. Paul, MN	1955	1754	2102	663	1361	1691	1334	3125		2005	574	3207
New York, NY	2843	301	1574	1353	3002	1971	2048	4500	2005		2121	4877
Omaha, NE	1397	1870	1475	763	867	1397	978	2685	574	2121		2756
San Francisco, CA	2869	4626	3847	3519	2034	3498	3255	652	3207	4877	2756	

Note: TX means Texas; MD means Maryland; etc.

1 What is the title of this chart? _____
(14)

2 In what order are the cities listed? _____
(15)
Look at the first letter of each city.

3 Do the numbers in the chart represent miles or kilometers?

_____
(16)

4 How far is it from Mpls-St. Paul to Omaha? _____ km
(17)

HINT
Find Mpls-St. Paul on the side of the chart.

Find Omaha on the top of the chart.

Move your fingers along the lines until they meet. This is the distance.

© 1983 by Dale Seymour Publications

Use the chart on page 3 to finish these problems.

You'll find this answer at the bottom of page 3.

FROM	TO	KILOMETERS
Mpls-St. Paul, MN	Omaha, NE	574
Chicago, IL	Mpls-St. Paul, MN	(18)
New York, NY	Baltimore, MD	(19)
Jackson, MS	Mpls-St. Paul, MN	(20)
San Francisco, CA	Los Angeles, CA	(21)
Birmingham, AL	Austin, TX	(22)
Mpls-St. Paul, MN	Baltimore, MD	(23)
Mpls-St. Paul, MN	Denver, CO	(24)
San Francisco, CA	Denver, CO	(25)
Birmingham, AL	Little Rock, AR	(26)
Austin, TX	Baltimore, MD	(27)
Los Angeles, CA	New York, NY	(28)

✳ How many kilometers would it be for a trip from Chicago to San Francisco with a stopover in Austin?

Chicago to Austin	_____	km
	(29)	
Austin to San Francisco	_____	km
	(30)	
Total trip	_____	km
	(31)	

© 1983 by Dale Seymour Publications   Road Distances   4

U.S. Road Distances (kilometers)	Albuquerque, NM	Cleveland, OH	Denver, CO	Houston, TX	Lansing, MI	Milwaukee, WI	Minneapolis, MN	Portland, OR	Tampa, FL	Washington, D.C.
Albuquerque, NM		2528	681	1334	2373	2158	1973	2277	2780	2970
Cleveland, OH	2528		2198	2084	352	690	1200	3973	1829	565
Denver, CO	681	2198		1651	2029	1612	1361	2068	2949	2751
Houston, TX	1334	2084	1651		2014	1873	1912	3596	1577	2283
Lansing, MI	2373	352	2029	2014		526	1030	3809	1928	898
Milwaukee, WI	2158	690	1612	1873	526		528	3303	2026	1244
Minneapolis, MN	1973	1200	1361	1912	1030	528		2741	2568	1744
Portland, OR	2277	3973	2068	3596	3809	3303	2741		4993	4526
Tampa, FL	2780	1829	2949	1577	1928	2026	2568	4993		1521
Washington, D.C.	2970	565	2751	2283	898	1244	1744	4526	1521	

1 How many kilometers is a trip from Albuquerque to Denver to Portland?

Albuquerque to Denver _____ km (32)

Denver to Portland _____ km (33)

Total trip _____ km (34)

2 How many kilometers is a trip from Houston to Milwaukee to Cleveland and back to Houston?

Houston to Milwaukee _____ (35)

Milwaukee to Cleveland _____ (36)

Cleveland to Houston _____ (37)

Total trip _____ (38)

Don't forget the units.

3 Minneapolis to Lansing to Cleveland to Tampa. Total distance is _____. (39)

4 Washington D.C. to Tampa to Houston to Portland. Total distance is _____. (40)

© 1983 by Dale Seymour Publications

Another type of road distance chart lists the names of the cities only once. Look at this chart:

Road Distances in Minnesota   (kilometers)

From \ To	Brainerd	Duluth	Ely	Grand Rapids	Hibbing	Int'l Falls	Mankato	Minneapolis	Northfield	Owatonna	Rochester	St. Cloud	St. Paul	Shakopee	Stillwater	Winona
Alexandria	138	322	442	256	327	394	265	211	275	315	344	111	228	227	245	404
Brainerd		183	304	134	188	312	288	201	265	306	335	103	211	214	228	388
Duluth			182	132	124	262	365	241	294	346	360	228	237	277	238	414
Ely				172	116	191	513	389	442	494	508	377	385	425	386	562
Grand Rapids					56	187	389	278	343	383	412	230	288	299	293	465
Hibbing						163	428	304	362	409	428	278	304	339	306	479
International Falls							576	465	521	570	587	414	463	486	465	640
Mankato								124	90	68	130	187	134	90	164	204
Minneapolis									64	105	134	105	14	35	42	190
Northfield										48	93	169	58	64	88	171
Owatonna											64	209	106	100	137	138
Rochester												238	124	142	140	74
St. Cloud													119	121	134	296
St. Paul														45	31	177
Shakopee															74	201
Stillwater																185

International Falls to St. Paul is 463 kilometers.

To find distances on this type of chart, find both cities on the chart. Move your finger straight across on the top city and up for the other city. The distance between the cities is found where your fingers meet.

1 What is the distance from Grand Rapids to Shakopee? _____ km
(41)

2 How far is it from Minneapolis to St. Paul? _____ km
(42)

3 From Northfield to St. Cloud is _____ kilometers.
(43)

© 1983 by Dale Seymour Publications

Use the chart on page 6 to finish these problems.

4 How far is it from Hibbing to International Falls? _____ km
(44)
How far is it from International Falls to Minneapolis? _____ km
(45)

5 Is the distance from Hibbing to International Falls to Minneapolis more or less than the distance from Hibbing straight to Minneapolis?

_____
(46)

Use problem 4 to help answer this.

6 Speedy Whiz is driving from her home in Minneapolis to visit her cousin in Duluth. How many kilometers will her trip be?
_____ km
(47)

7 Brainerd to St. Cloud is _____ kilometers.
(48)

8 According to the chart, what city is <u>closest</u> to Northfield? _____
(49)

Hint: Find Northfield in the chart, then look at the row of numbers to the right and the column of numbers up from Northfield. Find the smallest number and the town that corresponds to it.

9 What city is <u>farthest</u> from Minneapolis? _____
(50)
How far away is it? _____
(51)

10 What city is <u>closest</u> to Minneapolis? _____
(52)

11 How many kilometers is a trip from Minneapolis to Winona and <u>back</u>? _____
(53)

This is a <u>round</u> trip

12 Find these <u>round trips</u>:

Northfield to Rochester <u>and back</u> _____
(54)
St. Cloud to Ely <u>and back</u> _____
(55)
Alexandria to Duluth <u>and back</u> _____
(56)

© 1983 by Dale Seymour Publications

Give them a 'cm' and they will take a

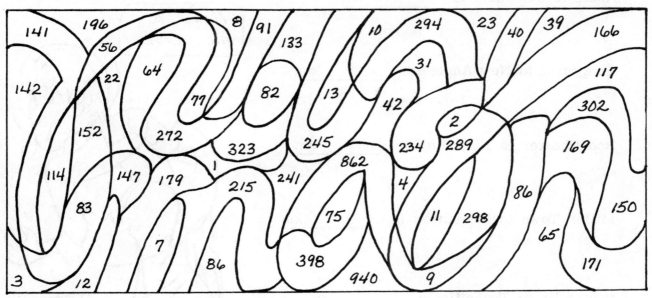

ROAD DISTANCES (kilometers)

	86	200	275	169	203	245	165	131	171	196	214	69	142	141	152	251
		114	189	83	117	194	179	125	165	190	208	64	131	133	142	241
			113	82	77	163	227	150	183	215	224	142	147	172	148	257
				107	72	119	319	242	275	307	316	234	239	264	240	349
					35	116	242	173	213	238	256	143	179	186	182	289
						101	266	189	225	254	266	173	189	211	190	298
							358	289	324	354	365	257	288	302	289	398
								77	56	42	81	116	83	56	102	127
									40	65	83	65	9	22	26	118
										30	58	105	36	40	55	106
											40	130	66	62	85	86
												148	77	88	87	46
													74	75	83	184
														28	19	110
															46	125
																115

Cities (diagonal labels): Acute · Applapolis · Arabesque · Congruent · Daisyville · Indyapolis · Jumpkins · Kiloville · Larkington · Literton · Measurton · Miller Town · New Angle · New Yogurt · Rod Chester · Square Corners · Teakettle

*
Use this chart to find the distance in each problem on the next page. Then shade each area in the puzzle above that contains an answer.

© 1983 by Dale Seymour Publications

Road Distances   8

Acute to Jumpkins is _____ km

Congruent to New Angle is _____ km

Rod Chester to Kiloville is _____ km

Miller Town to Measurton is _____ km

Indyapolis to Teakettle is _____ km

Arabesque to New Yogurt and back is _____ km

Daisyville to Applapolis and back is _____ km

Square Corners to Larkington and then to New Angle is _____ km

Literton to Miller Town and then to Acute is _____ km

Arabesque to Kiloville to Rod Chester and then to Literton is _____ km

What is the distance to the town closest to Larkington? _____ km

What is the distance to the town farthest from Square Corners? _____ km

© 1983 by Dale Seymour Publications

NAME _____

U.S. ROAD DISTANCES (kilometers)	Austin, TX	Baltimore, MD	Birmingham, AL	Chicago, IL	Denver, CO	Jackson, MS	Little Rock, AR	Los Angeles, CA	Mpls-St. Paul, MN	New York, NY	Omaha, NE	San Francisco, CA
Austin, TX		2529	1257	1823	1459	861	795	2227	1955	2843	1397	2869
Baltimore, MD	2529		1273	1102	2624	1670	1752	4262	1754	301	1870	4626
Birmingham, AL	1257	1273		1051	2095	397	632	3319	2102	1574	1475	3847
Chicago, IL	1823	1102	1051		1630	1212	1046	3366	663	1353	763	3519
Denver, CO	1459	2624	2095	1630		1923	1553	1862	1361	3002	867	2034
Jackson, MS	861	1670	397	1212	1923		418	2922	1691	1971	1397	3498
Little Rock, AR	795	1752	632	1046	1553	418		2727	1334	2048	978	3255
Los Angeles, CA	2227	4262	3319	3366	1862	2922	2727		3125	4500	2685	652
Mpls-St. Paul, MN	1955	1754	2102	663	1361	1691	1334	3125		2005	574	3207
New York, NY	2843	301	1574	1353	3002	1971	2048	4500	2005		2121	4877
Omaha, NE	1397	1870	1475	763	867	1397	978	2685	574	2121		2756
San Francisco, CA	2869	4626	3847	3519	2034	3498	3255	652	3207	4877	2756	

1. How far is it from Austin to San Francisco? _____ km

2. Which city is farther from Mpls-St. Paul: Los Angeles or New York?

    _____

3. What town on the chart is closest to Denver? _____

    What is the distance from this town to Denver? _____ km

4. How many kilometers would it be for a trip from Denver to Mpls-St. Paul

    to Chicago?

    Denver to Mpls-St. Paul _____ km

    Mpls-St. Paul to Chicago _____ km

    Total trip _____ km

© 1983 by Dale Seymour Publications

Road Distances in Minnesota (kilometers)

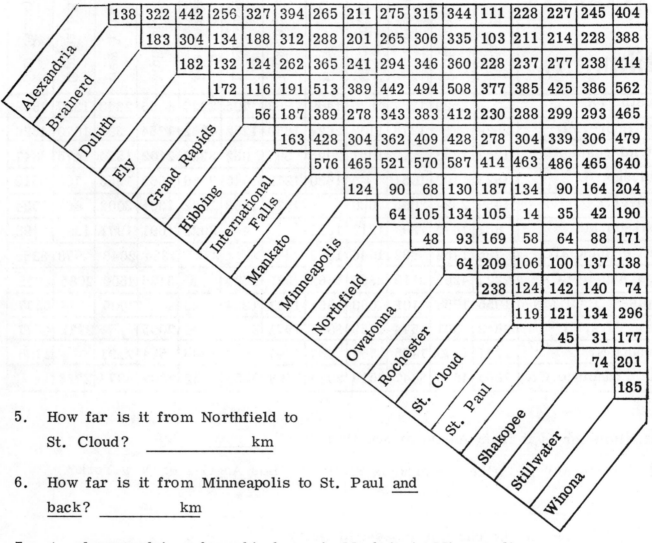

	Alexandria	Brainerd	Duluth	Ely	Grand Rapids	Hibbing	International Falls	Mankato	Minneapolis	Northfield	Owatonna	Rochester	St. Cloud	St. Paul	Shakopee	Stillwater	Winona
Alexandria	138	322	442	256	327	394	265	211	275	315	344	111	228	227	245	404
Brainerd		183	304	134	188	312	288	201	265	306	335	103	211	214	228	388
Duluth			182	132	124	262	365	241	294	346	360	228	237	277	238	414
Ely				172	116	191	513	389	442	494	508	377	385	425	386	562
Grand Rapids					56	187	389	278	343	383	412	230	288	299	293	465
Hibbing						163	428	304	362	409	428	278	304	339	306	479
International Falls							576	465	521	570	587	414	463	486	465	640
Mankato								124	90	68	130	187	134	90	164	204
Minneapolis									64	105	134	105	14	35	42	190
Northfield										48	93	169	58	64	88	171
Owatonna											64	209	106	100	137	138
Rochester												238	124	142	140	74
St. Cloud													119	121	134	296
St. Paul														45	31	177
Shakopee															74	201
Stillwater																185

5. How far is it from Northfield to
St. Cloud? _____ km

6. How far is it from Minneapolis to St. Paul <u>and</u>
<u>back</u>? _____ km

7. A salesman drives from his home in Mankato to Minneapolis,
then to Northfield, and then home. How far did he travel?
_____ km

8. What town on the chart is <u>closest</u> to Stillwater? _____

© 1983 by Dale Seymour Publications   Road Distances   T2

1. Distances for Arithem County
2. kilometers
3. 75
4. 45
5. 39
6. 106
7. 30
8. 25
9. 55
10. 39
11. 30
12. 69
13. 26
14. U.S. Road Distances
15. alphabetical
16. kilometers
17. 574
18. 663
19. 301
20. 1691
21. 652
22. 1257
23. 1754
24. 1361
25. 2034

26. 632
27. 2529
28. 4500
29. 1823
30. 2869
31. 4692
32. 681
33. 2068
34. 2749
35. 1873 km
36. 690 km
37. 2084 km
38. 4647 km
39. 3211 km
40. 6694 km
41. 299
42. 14
43. 169
44. 163
45. 465
46. more
47. 241
48. 103
49. Owatonna
50. International Falls

© 1983 by Dale Seymour Publications

51. _465_
52. _St. Paul_
53. _380 km_
54. _186 km_
55. _754 km_
56. _644 km_

PUZZLE ANSWER
page 8 (Shading puzzle):

km

(turn the page upside down)

© 1983 by Dale Seymour Publications

general math project

minneapolis public schools

UNIT: TRAVEL TIPS

DESCRIPTION: The students practice looking at maps
and estimating distances.

SKILLS TO BE REINFORCED: estimation skills

PREREQUISITE SKILLS: taking half of a number
doubling a number

LENGTH: four pages;   one day

TEACHER NOTES: The unit ROAD DISTANCES deals with maps, mileage
charts and exact distances. It could be used either before or
after TRAVEL TIPS.

NO TEST

© 1983 by Dale Seymour Publications

TRAVEL TIPS

You don't always need to know a distance exactly.
If you know some distances, you can ESTIMATE others.

Look at the map below.

★ The distance between Chicago and New York is about ____**?**____ the distance between Chicago and Minneapolis.

Would you choose <u>half</u>, <u>twice</u> or <u>the same as</u> to finish this sentence?

> There are several ways to estimate distances on a map. You can line up the distances on a ruler, a piece of paper, a string or your finger. You can even just "eyeball" the distance.

★ The distance between Chicago and New York is about <u>twice</u> the distance between Chicago and Minneapolis.

Chicago to Minneapolis is about 650 km.

So, Chicago to New York is about twice that, or about _____ km.
(1)

UNITED STATES

© 1983 by Dale Seymour Publications

Using the map on page 1, do the following. Use a ruler or just estimate by sight. Circle the best answer for part A. Fill in the blank for part B.

A.   The distance between Denver and Minneapolis is about _____ as the distance between Chicago and Minneapolis.

half as far   the same   twice as far   (2)

B.   The distance between Chicago and Minneapolis is about 650 km.
About how far is it from Denver to Minneapolis? _____ km.
(3)

A.   The distance between Seattle and Denver is about _____ as the distance between Los Angeles and New York.

half as far   the same   twice as far   (4)

B.   The distance between Los Angeles and New York is about 4500 km.
About how far is it from Seattle to Denver? _____ km.
(5)

A.   The distance between Minneapolis and New Orleans is about _____ as the distance between San Francisco and Los Angeles.

the same   twice as far   three times as far (6)

B.   The distance between San Francisco and Los Angeles is about
650 km. About how far is it from Minneapolis to New Orleans?
_____ km.
(7)

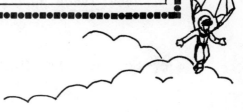

© 1983 by Dale Seymour Publications

Travel Tips 2

MINNESOTA

How far is it from Two Harbors to Grand Marais if the distance from Cloquet to Two Harbors is about 70 km?

★ The distance from Two Harbors to Grand Marais appears to be about <u>twice</u> as far as the distance from Cloquet to Two Harbors.

★ So, from Two Harbors to Grand Marais should be about _____ km.
(B)

© 1983 by Dale Seymour Publications

> Use the map on page 3 to do these.

> Distances used on this page are "as the crow flies" – that is, in a straight line.

＊ Part A: Circle the correct answer.
Part B: Fill in the blank.

1 The distance from Cloquet to Minneapolis is <u>about</u> 200 km. Estimate the distance from Minneapolis to Walnut Grove.

A. about half as far   about the same   about twice as far   (9)

B. about _____ km
___(10)___

2 From Rochester to Minneapolis it is about 120 km. <u>About</u> how far is it from Worthington to Minneapolis?

A. about half as far   about the same   about twice as far   (11)

B. about _____ km
___(12)___

3 It takes about two and one half hours to travel from Worthington to Benson. Going the same speed, <u>about</u> how long would it take to travel from Worthington to Warroad?

A.
about
twice as long

about
three times as long

about
four times as long

B. about _____ hours
___(14)___

- -

4 How far is it from Warroad to Cass Lake if the distance from Little Falls to Bemidji is about 170 km? about _____
___(15)___

5 How far is it from Cass Lake to Sandstone if the distance from Cloquet to Sandstone is about 70 km? about _____
___(16)___

6 If it takes about two hours to travel from Grand Marais to Cloquet, how long would it take to travel from Grand Marais to Cloquet to Little Falls to Austin?

about _____
___(17)___

© 1983 by Dale Seymour Publications   Travel Tips 4

1. 1300
2. *twice as far*
3. 1300
4. *half as far*
5. 2250
6. *three times as far*
7. 1950
8. 140
9. *about the same*
10. 200
11. *about twice as far*
12. 240
13. *about three times as long*
14. 7.5
15. *170 km*
16. *210 km*
17. *8 hours*
18. _____
19. _____
20. _____
21. _____
22. _____
23. _____
24. _____
25. _____
26. _____
27. _____
28. _____
29. _____
30. _____
31. _____
32. _____
33. _____
34. _____
35. _____
36. _____
37. _____
38. _____
39. _____
40. _____
41. _____
42. _____
43. _____
44. _____
45. _____
46. _____
47. _____
48. _____
49. _____
50. _____

© 1983 by Dale Seymour Publications

gmp

general math project

minneapolis public schools

UNIT: DAY FINDER

DESCRIPTION: This unit explains how to use the Day Finder Formula to find the day of the week on which a particular date falls.

SKILLS TO BE REINFORCED: using a formula by following a step-by-step procedure

division of whole numbers with remainders

PREREQUISITE SKILLS: ability to read dates given in different forms

assigning the correct number to a given month

using a chart

whole number addition

LENGTH: 9 pages; 2-3 days

TEACHER NOTES: If the students have difficulty with this unit, pages 7-8 can be omitted. You may also wish to allow calculator use after the first few pages.

The formula and charts are reproduced on the last page of the unit for easy reference.

The next unit, IS IT YOUR DAY?, uses remainders in a similar manner to solve biorhythm problems.

NO TEST

© 1983 by Dale Seymour Publications

Day Finder

Monday's child
   is fair of face,
Tuesday's child
   is full of grace,
Wednesday's child
   is full of woe,
Thursday's child
   has far to go,
Friday's child
   is loving and giving,
Saturday's child
   works hard for a living,
And the child that is born
   on the Sabbath day
Is bonny and blithe and good every way.

Do you know...

on what day of the week you were born?

on what day of the week you will be 18?

on what day of the week Jan. 1, 2000, will fall?

You can find the answers to these questions if you use the formula that we call the . . .

DAY FINDER FORMULA: $\left(\dfrac{Y}{4} + MC + D + Y \right) \div 7$

To use this formula, you need to know how to tell the month, day and year in any date.

July 4, 1976   7-4-76   7/4/76   4 July 76

These all represent the fourth day in the month of July in the year 1976.

✱ For each date below, give the <u>month</u>, <u>day</u> and <u>last two digits</u> of the year.

September 4, 1948

Month _Sept._ Day _4_ Year _48_

May 22, 1924

Month ____ Day ____ Year ____ (1)

2/11/37

Month _Feb._ Day ____ Year ____ (2)

1 November 71

Month ____ Day ____ Year ____ (3)

6 - 10 - 76

Month ____ Day ____ Year ____ (4)

13 August 80

Month ____ Day ____ Year ____ (5)

© 1983 by Dale Seymour Publications

Now look at the Day Finder Formula again:

$$\left(\frac{Y}{4} + MC + D + Y \right) \div 7$$

For any given date . . .

    MC   is the <u>M</u>onth <u>C</u>ode from this chart

    D   is the <u>D</u>ay of the month

    Y   is the <u>last two digits</u> of the <u>Y</u>ear

✻ Find the Month Code for each of these dates:

MONTH CODE CHART	
January = 1	if a Leap Year, 0
February = 4	if a Leap Year, 3
March = 4	
April = 0	
May = 2	
June = 5	
July = 0	
August = 3	
September = 6	
October = 1	
November = 4	
December = 6	

July 15, 1972   Month = _____ so, MC = _____ (6)

11-19-77   Month = _____ so, MC = _____ (7)

9/26/75   Month = _____ so, MC = _____ (8)

6 June 81   Month = _____ so, MC = _____ (9)

✻ Now fill in the formula for each given date.

| April 7, 1982 | For this date; MC = _0_, D = _7_, Y = 82 *(Last two digits only)*

and the Formula is $\left(\dfrac{\;\;\;\;}{4} + \underline{\quad} + \underline{\quad} + \underline{\quad} \right) \div 7$ (10)
$\qquad\qquad\qquad\quad (Y)\qquad\quad (MC)\quad\; (D)\quad\;\; (Y)$

| 3/27/69 | For this date; MC = _____, D = _____, Y = _____ (11)

and the Formula is $\left(\dfrac{\;\;\;\;}{4} + \underline{\quad} + \underline{\quad} + \underline{\quad} \right) \div 7$ (12)

| 10-31-68 | For this date; MC = _____, D = _____, Y = _____ (13)

and the Formula is $\left(\dfrac{\;\;\;\;}{4} + \underline{\quad} + \underline{\quad} + \underline{\quad} \right) \div 7$ (14)

| 17 May 55 | For this date; MC = _____, D = _____, Y = _____ (15)

and the Formula is $\left(\dfrac{\;\;\;\;}{4} + \underline{\quad} + \underline{\quad} + \underline{\quad} \right) \div 7$ (16)

© 1983 by Dale Seymour Publications

Now let's actually figure out the day for a given date using the Day Finder Formula: $\left(\frac{Y}{4} + MC + D + Y\right) \div 7$

Neil Armstrong was the first person to set foot on the moon on July 21, 1969. What day of the week was it? For July 21, 1969; MC=___, D=___, Y=___ and (17)

$\left(\dfrac{Y}{4} + MC + D + Y\right) \div 7$ is $\left(\dfrac{69}{4} + \underline{\hspace{1cm}} + \underline{\hspace{1cm}} + \underline{\hspace{1cm}}\right) \div 7$ (18)

To find the answer, follow these steps:

1 Divide $\dfrac{Y}{4} = \dfrac{69}{4}$ to get the answer <u>without</u> the remainder.

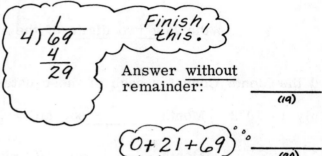

Finish this!

Answer <u>without</u> remainder: _____ (19)

2 Add together MC + D + Y

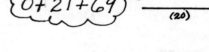

$(0 + 21 + 69)$ _____ (20)

3 Add the answers from steps 1 and 2. This is $\left(\dfrac{Y}{4} + MC + D + Y\right)$ in the Formula. Call it the TOTAL:

(21)

4 Divide this TOTAL by 7. This time you want <u>only</u> the REMAINDER!

REMAINDER: _____ (22)

5 Now, in this chart, find the REMAINDER. This tells the day of the week.

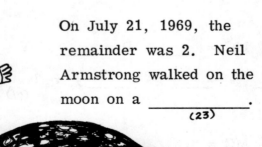

On July 21, 1969, the remainder was 2. Neil Armstrong walked on the moon on a _____ . (23)

DAY CHART

0 = Saturday

1 = Sunday

2 = Monday

3 = Tuesday

4 = Wednesday

5 = Thursday

6 = Friday

© 1983 by Dale Seymour Publications

✳ Mount St. Helens, a volcano in Washington, erupted for the first time in over one hundred years on 5-18-80. What day of the week was that?

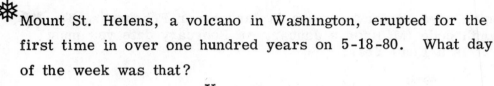

$$\left(\frac{Y}{4} + MC + D + Y \right) \div 7 \quad is$$

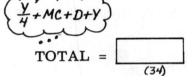

$$\left(\frac{}{4} + \underline{} + \underline{} + \underline{} \right) \div 7$$
(24)

Follow the steps on page 3.

Page 9 contains the charts needed for the Day Finder Formula; use page 9 for reference as you work through the unit.

1 Divide $\frac{Y}{4}$ to get the answer **without** the remainder. $4\overline{)}$ Answer **without** remainder: _____ (25)

2 Add $MC + D + Y$ = _____ + _____ + _____ = _____ (27)
(26)

3 Add the answers from steps 1 and 2.   TOTAL: [ ] (28)

4 Divide this **TOTAL** by 7 and get the **REMAINDER**. $7\overline{)}$ REMAINDER: _____ (29)

5 Find the REMAINDER in the Day Chart. *see page 9*

5-18-80 was a _____ (30)

★ Eric Heiden, winner of five gold medals at the 1980 Winter Olympics, was born 14 October 58. What day of the week was that?

$$\left(\frac{Y}{4} + MC + D + Y \right) \div 7 \quad is \quad \left(\frac{}{4} + \underline{} + \underline{} + \underline{} \right) \div \underline{}$$
(31)

answer without remainder

$\frac{Y}{4}$ = _____ ; $MC + D + Y$ = _____ ; $\frac{Y}{4}+MC+D+Y$ TOTAL = [ ]
(32)   (33)   (34)

Now, divide the TOTAL by 7 and get the REMAINDER: _____
(35)

14 October 58 was a _____ (36)

© 1983 by Dale Seymour Publications

✱ None of the dates you've used so far has been in January or February. To ✱ choose the proper month code (MC) for a January or February date you must know whether or not it is a Leap Year.

A year is a Leap Year if...

The last 2 digits are not both zeroes and the year is evenly divisible by 4.	The last 2 digits are both zeroes and the year is evenly divisible by 400.
1980 is a Leap Year.	**1600** is a Leap Year.

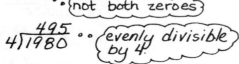

not both zeroes

$$4\overline{)1980}\ \ \overset{495}{}$$ *(evenly divisible by 4.)*

both zeroes

$$400\overline{)1600}\ \ \overset{40}{}$$ *(evenly divisible by 400)*

Write YES or NO to tell if each year is a Leap Year.

1754 ____ (37)   1939 ____ (39)   2020 ____ (41)   1976 ____ (43)

1812 ____ (38)   1700 ____ (40)   2000 ____ (42)   1845 ____ (44)

Now let's go back to the Day Finder Formula

✱ On what day will 1-1-84 fall?

This is a January date. Is 1984 a LEAP YEAR? _____ (45)

(Use the Jan. Leap Year month code)

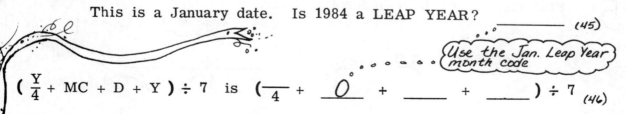

$$\left(\frac{Y}{4} + MC + D + Y\right) \div 7 \text{ is } \left(\frac{}{4} + \underline{\ 0\ } + \underline{} + \underline{}\right) \div 7 \ (46)$$

Use the same steps to find the answer as you did before: 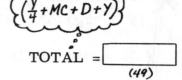 $\left(\frac{Y}{4}+MC+D+Y\right)$

answer without remainder

$$\frac{Y}{4} = \underline{} (47) \qquad MC + D + Y = \underline{} (48) \qquad \text{TOTAL} = \boxed{} (49)$$

Now, divide the TOTAL by 7 and get the remainder: ____ (50)

1 - 1 - 84   is   a   _____ (51)

HAPPY NEW YEAR

© 1983 by Dale Seymour Publications

Now work these problems. For a January or February date, be sure to see if it falls in a Leap Year and then use the correct month code.

On what day of the week did the Bicentennial fall (7/4/76) ?

_____
(52)

Willy Merri and Ida Wana decide to get married on February 14, 1990. What day of the week will that be? _____
(53)

The coldest recorded temperature was -126.9° F on 24 August 60, in Vostok, Antarctica. What day of the week was it?

_____
(54)

Orville and Wilbur Wright were the first to fly a power driven airplane on December 17, 1903. What day of the week was it? _____
(55)

On what date will you turn 18? _____
(56)
On what day of the week will you turn 18?

_____
(57)

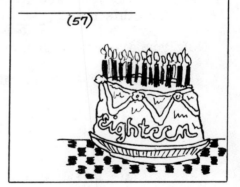

What is your birthdate? _____ Use the Day Finder Formula to
(58)
figure out on what day of the week you were born. _____
(59)

© 1983 by Dale Seymour Publications   Day Finder   6

There are two situations in which you must take some other steps before you use the Day Finder Formula.

1 You must check to see if January and February dates fall in a Leap Year, and then use the correct month code in the Formula.

2 You must change the Formula slightly before you can find the days for dates in centuries other than the 1900's.

For centuries other than the 1900's, add the appropriate number to the Day Finder Formula before dividing by 7.	CENTURY	ADD	
	1700's	4	*add 2 here*
	1800's	2 .....$(\frac{Y}{4}+MC+D+Y+\underline{2})\div 7$	
	1900's	0	
	2000's	-1	*add -3 here*
	2100's	-3 .....$(\frac{Y}{4}+MC+D+Y-\underline{3})\div 7$	

Now try these:

① July 4, 1776, fell on what day?

Is this a century other than the 1900's? _____ (60)

If so, what century number do you add? _____ (61)

Do you have to also check to see if 1776 is a Leap Year for this date? _____ (62) Why or why not? _____ (63)

Now you are ready to use the Formula:

For July 4, 1776, it is: $(\dfrac{}{4} + \underline{} + \underline{} + \underline{} + \underline{}) \div 7$ (64)

$$\frac{Y}{4} = \underline{}\ \ (65) \quad \text{\textit{answer without remainder}}$$

MC + D + Y + 4 = _____ (66)

$(\frac{Y}{4}+MC+D+Y+4)$ ....TOTAL = [   ] (67)

Divide the TOTAL by 7 and get the remainder: _____ (68)

July 4, 1776, was a _____ (69)

© 1983 by Dale Seymour Publications

② Abraham Lincoln was born on February 12, 1809. What day of the week was this?

Is this a century other than the 1900's? _____ (70)

If so, what is added to the Formula? _____ (71)

Do you have to check to see if 1809 is a Leap Year? _____ Is it? _____
(72)   (73)

For February 12, 1809, the Formula is:

$$(\frac{}{4} + \underline{} + \underline{} + \underline{} + \underline{}) \div 7$$
(74)

century number

no remainder

$$\frac{Y}{4} = \underline{}$$
(75)

$$MC + D + Y + \underline{} = \underline{}$$
(76)

$$TOTAL = \boxed{}$$
(77)

Now, divide the TOTAL by 7 and get the remainder: _____
(78)

February 12, 1809, was a _____
(79)

③ January 1, 2000, will fall on what day?

For this date, the Formula is:

$$(\frac{00}{4} + \underline{} + \underline{} + \underline{} + \underline{}) \div 7$$
(80)

leap year?   *century number*

$$\frac{Y}{4} = \underline{}$$
(81)

$$MC + D + Y - 1 = \underline{}$$
(82)

$$TOTAL = \boxed{}$$
(83)

Now, divide the TOTAL by 7 and get the remainder: _____
(84)

January 1, 2000 will, be a _____
(85)

④ If you lived to be 100, on what day of the week would your birthday be? _____
(86)

© 1983 by Dale Seymour Publications

DAY FINDER REFERENCE PAGE

DAY FINDER FORMULA: $\left(\frac{Y}{4} + MC + D + Y \right) \div 7$

MONTH CODE CHART

January = 1   if a Leap Year, 0

February = 4   if a Leap Year, 3

March = 4

April = 0

May = 2

June = 5

July = 0

August = 3

September = 6

October = 1

November = 4

December = 6

DAY CHART

0 = Saturday

1 = Sunday

2 = Monday

3 = Tuesday

4 = Wednesday

5 = Thursday

6 = Friday

- -

CENTURY CHART

CENTURY	ADD
1700's	4
1800's	2
1900's	0
2000's	-1
2100's	-3

used only on pages 7 & 8

© 1983 by Dale Seymour Publications

1. May 22 24
2. Feb. 11 37
3. Nov. 1 71
4. June 10 76
5. Aug. 13 80
6. July 0
7. Nov. 4
8. Sept. 6
9. June 5
10. $\left(\frac{82}{4} + 0 + 7 + 82\right)$
11. MC=4, D=27, Y=69
12. $\left(\frac{69}{4} + 4 + 27 + 69\right)$
13. MC=1, D=31, Y=68
14. $\left(\frac{68}{4} + 1 + 31 + 68\right)$
15. MC=2, D=17, Y=55
16. $\left(\frac{55}{4} + 2 + 17 + 55\right)$
17. MC=0, D=21, Y=69
18. $\left(\frac{69}{4} + 0 + 21 + 69\right)$
19. 17
20. 90
21. 107
22. 2
23. Monday
24. $\left(\frac{80}{4} + 2 + 18 + 80\right)$
25. 20

26. 2+18+80
27. 100
28. 120
29. 1
30. Sunday
31. $\left(\frac{58}{4} + 1 + 14 + 58\right) \div 7$
32. 14
33. 73
34. 87
35. 3
36. Tuesday
37. No
38. Yes
39. No
40. No
41. Yes
42. Yes
43. Yes
44. No
45. Yes
46. $\left(\frac{84}{4} + 0 + 1 + 84\right)$
47. 21
48. 85
49. 106
50. 1

51. *Sunday*
52. *Sunday*
53. *Wednesday*
54. *Wednesday*
55. *Thursday*
56. *answers will vary*
57. *answers will vary*
58. *answers will vary*
59. *answers will vary*
60. *Yes*
61. *4*
62. *No*
63. *not a Jan. or Feb. date*
64. $\left(\frac{76}{4} + 0 + 4 + 76 + 4\right)$
65. *19*
66. *84*
67. *103*
68. *5*
69. *Thursday*
70. *Yes*
71. *2*
72. *Yes*
73. *No*
74. $\left(\frac{9}{4} + 4 + 12 + 9 + 2\right)$
75. *2*

76. $MC + D + Y + 2 = 27$
77. *29*
78. *1*
79. *Sunday*
80. $\left(\frac{00}{4} + 0 + 1 + 00 + -1\right)$
81. *0*
82. *0*
83. *0*
84. *0*
85. *Saturday*
86. *answers will vary*
87.
88.
89.
90.
91.
92.
93.
94.
95.
96.
97.
98.
99.
100.

© 1983 by Dale Seymour Publications

general math project

minneapolis public schools

UNIT: IS IT YOUR DAY?

DESCRIPTION: In this unit, the students learn what the biorhythm
theory is and then find their own biorhythm cycles.

SKILLS TO BE REINFORCED: division of whole numbers

ability to follow step-by-step instructions

PREREQUISITE SKILLS: ability to read a graph

addition of whole numbers

LENGTH: seven pages;   three or four days

TEACHER NOTES: Here are some references for those who want to
pursue the subject:

Bolch, Jennifer, "Biorhythms: A Key to Your Ups
and Downs", Reader's Digest, Sept., 1977, p. 63.
Kalterborn, Bonnie, "Your Biorhythm and the Sine
Curve", The Mathematics Teacher, Oct., 1977,
pp. 581-83.

If your school has a computer terminal, you could
inquire as to whether or not there is a program to
find biorhythms.   (In Mpls. GET - *BOSIN explains
the biorhythm theory and will find a person's
biorhythm graph for a given number of days.   On
APPLE, there is a program on biorhythms also.)

It would be helpful to put the three curves on the
board or on a chart for easy access at a glance.

A calculator is useful in some parts.

NO TEST

© 1983 by Dale Seymour Publications

Is It Your Day?

The Biorhythm Theory <u>claims</u> to be able to help you answer this question.

A theory is an idea which some people believe and others don't. It is an idea which has not been proved to be absolutely right or wrong.

The Biorhythm Theory states that our bodies and minds have cycles which rule the way we feel, behave and think. These cycles begin at birth and repeat themselves until death. The Biorhythm Theory states that there are 3 repeating cycles.

INTELLECTUAL: we vary from being able to think clearly and quickly to being mentally lazy and forgetful. This cycle repeats itself every 33 days.

PHYSICAL: we vary periodically from being energetic to being tired and lazy. This cycle repeats itself every 23 days.

EMOTIONAL: we vary from being cheerful and cooperative to being moody, sensitive and irritable. This is a 28 day cycle.

Cycles are usually shown in graph form. Each cycle is centered around a "zero line".

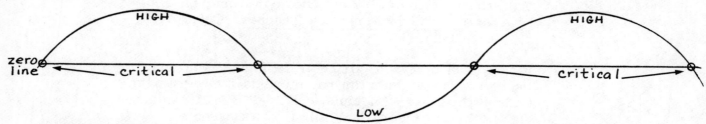

The Biorhythm Theory says . . .

* The high periods (above the zero line) are days when you have the most energy, are most cheerful, or are most alert.

* The low periods (below the zero line) are days of resting, moodiness or forgetfulness.

* The days where the graph crosses the zero line are called <u>critical days</u>! These are days when you are apt to cause accidents, make mistakes or maybe experience a tragedy. The day before and the day after a critical day are considered to be critical days also.

© 1983 by Dale Seymour Publications

People who believe in the Biorhythm Theory often look at the lives of celebrities, sports heroes or other public people and try to connect their successes or tragedies to points on their Biorhythm cycles.

For example:

* Clark Gable died of a heart attack on a **critical day**.

* Marilyn Monroe took a fatal dose of medicine on a **critical day**.

* Thomas Edison discovered the light bulb on a **positive day**.

* Sirhan Sirhan shot Bobby Kennedy on a **critical day**.

* Muhammad Ali lost a fight to Joe Frazier on March 8, 1971 . . .

Let's see if the Biorhythm Theory would have predicted Ali's loss.

* In order to use the Biorhythm **Theory** you need to know how many days a person has been alive on a given day.

Ali was born on January 19, 1942. On March 8, 1971, Ali had been alive 10,641 days. This includes the day he was born, leap year days and the day of the fight.

The next two pages will show you how to use this information to answer the question, "WAS MARCH 8, 1971, ALI'S DAY?"

© 1983 by Dale Seymour Publications

Intellectual Cycle

According to the Theory, every person has a 33 day Intellectual Cycle. To find out where Ali was intellectually on the day of the fight . . .

★ Divide the number of days he had been alive on that day (10,641) by 33. Use long division and no calculator because you need to find the <u>remainder</u>!

This should be a number smaller than 33

Remainder is ▭

(1)

★ Find the <u>remainder</u> on this graph of the Intellectual Cycle.

Find 15 on the zero line. Then draw a line straight up to the graph of the cycle.

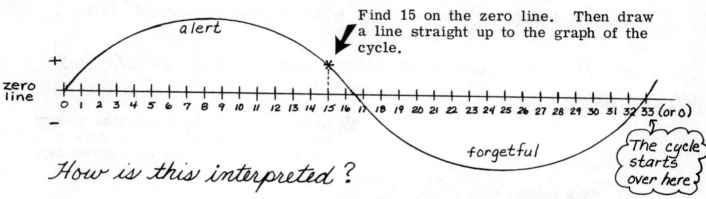

How is this interpreted?

According to the Biorhythm Theory for the INTELLECTUAL CYCLE:

✳ If the remainder is 0, 1, 16, 17 or 32, it is a critical day. Beware of making mistakes.

✳ If the remainder is from 2 to 15, a person is on the high part of the cycle. He or she is probably alert and able to think clearly.

Remember, these numbers only pertain to the graph of the Intellectual Cycle!

✳ If the remainder is from 18 to 31, a person is on the low part of the cycle. He or she may be somewhat forgetful and not very alert.

According to the graph, how should Ali have felt intellectually on March 8, 1971?

_____ .

(2)

© 1983 by Dale Seymour Publications

Physical Cycle

The Physical Cycle is repeated every 23 days.   To find out where Ali was physically on March 8, 1971 . . .

(The number of days Ali had lived.)

✸ Divide 10,641 by 23 and get the remainder!

(3)

✸ Find the remainder on the graph below.

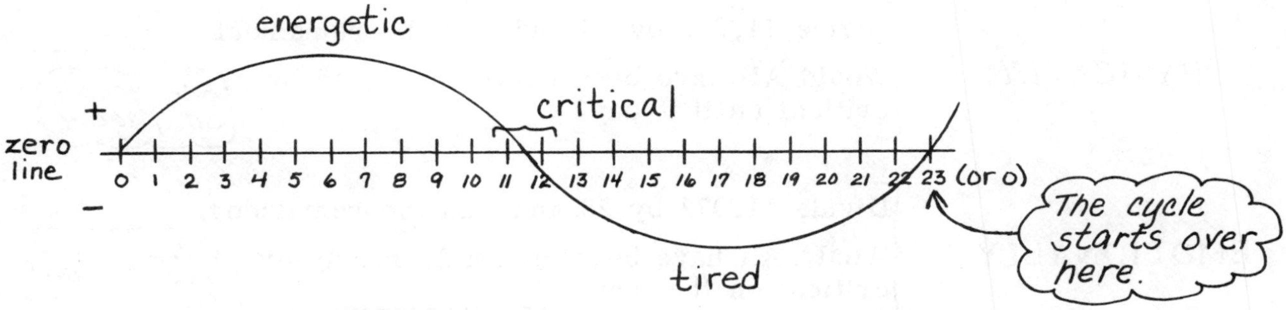

energetic

critical

zero line

+
-

0 1 2 3 4 5 6 7 8 9 10 11 12 13 14 15 16 17 18 19 20 21 22 23 (or 0)

tired

The cycle starts over here.

According to the graph, how should Ali have felt physically on March 8, 1971?

_____.

(4)

Emotional Cycle

The Emotional Cycle is repeated every 28 days.   To find out where Ali was emotionally on March 8, 1971 . . .

✸ Divide 10,641 by 28 and get the remainder!

(5)

✸ Now find the remainder on the graph below.

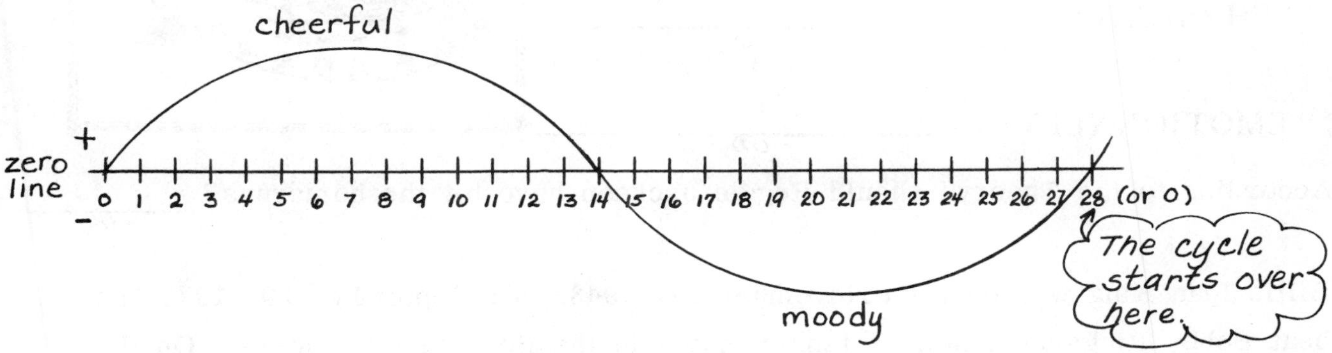

cheerful

zero line

+
-

0 1 2 3 4 5 6 7 8 9 10 11 12 13 14 15 16 17 18 19 20 21 22 23 24 25 26 27 28 (or 0)

moody

The cycle starts over here.

According to the graph, how should Ali have felt emotionally on March 8, 1971?

_____.

(6)

Looking at all 3 cycles, WAS IT ALI'S DAY? According to the Theory, should Ali have lost the fight? _____

(7)

© 1983 by Dale Seymour Publications   Is It Your Day? 4

Let's try another example using Muhammad Ali. Ali knocked out George Foreman on October 29, 1974. Ali had been alive 11,972 days on that day.

According to the Biorhythm Theory, what kind of day was Ali having . . .

INTELLECTUALLY:
Divide 11,972 by 33 and find the remainder. _____ (8)
Would Ali have been alert, forgetful or critical on that day? _____ (9) *see graph on page 3*

PHYSICALLY:
Divide 11,972 by 23 and find the remainder. _____ (10)
Would Ali have been energetic, tired or critical on that day? _____ (11) *see graph on page 4*

EMOTIONALLY:
Divide 11,972 by 28 and find the remainder. _____ (12)
Would Ali have been cheerful, moody or critical on that day? _____ (13) *see graph on page 4*

✱According to the Theory, should Ali have won the fight? _____ (14)

Reggie Jackson was born on May 18, 1946. On October 18, 1977, in game 6 of the World Series, Jackson hit 3 successive homeruns. On that day he had been living for 11,477 days.

According to the Biorhythm Theory, what kind of day was Jackson having . . .

INTELLECTUALLY: _____ (15)

PHYSICALLY: _____ (16)

EMOTIONALLY: _____ (17)

✱According to the Theory, should Reggie Jackson have hit the homeruns? _____ (18)

Billie Jean King was born on November 22, 1943. On September 20, 1973, she beat Bobby Riggs in a famous tennis match in the Houston Astrodome. On that day she had been living for 10,585 days.

✱According to the Theory, should Billie Jean King have won the tennis match? _____ (19)

© 1983 by Dale Seymour Publications

❋ In order to answer the question "IS IT YOUR DAY?", you must figure out how many days you have been alive on a given day.

Guess how many days you have been alive. _____
(20)

FOLLOW THESE 4 STEPS TO SEE HOW MANY DAYS YOU HAVE BEEN ALIVE.

(Use a calculator if you have one.)

Put your answers in the boxes.

1 Multiply your age at your last birthday by 365.

(21)

2 Count the number of these Leap Year days that you have been alive:

(22)

Feb. 29, 1956	Feb. 29, 1972
Feb. 29, 1960	Feb. 29, 1976
Feb. 29, 1964	Feb. 29, 1980
Feb. 29, 1968	Feb. 29, 1984

3 Now count the number of days from your last birthday to the present day. (Count the birthday and today.)

(23)

This chart may help

Jan.	31 days		July	31 days
Feb.	28 days (29 in Leap Year)		Aug.	31 days
Mar.	31 days		Sept.	30 days
Apr.	30 days		Oct.	31 days
May	31 days		Nov.	30 days
June	30 days		Dec.	31 days

4 Add the results from steps 1, 2, and 3.

(24)

This is the total number of days you have lived as of today.

© 1983 by Dale Seymour Publications

❋According to the Biorhythm Theory, how should you feel today?

INTELLECTUALLY: _____
(25)

PHYSICALLY: _____
(26)

EMOTIONALLY: _____
(27)

Use the graphs on pages 3 and 4.

Do you feel your actual day is going the way the Biorhythm Theory would predict it should? _____
(28)

This just hasn't been my day.

Do you think that the Biorhythm Theory is accurate? _____

_____

_____

_____

_____
(29)

Use examples from this unit to tell why or why not.

Figure out what your day will be like on your 21st birthday. Remember, there will be a leap year day on Feb. 29, 1984 and on Feb. 29, 1988.

_____
(30)

© 1983 by Dale Seymour Publications

UNIT _Is It Your Day?_ ANSWER KEY

1. 15
2. alert
3. 15
4. tired
5. 1
6. critical
7. yes, probably
8. 26
9. forgetful
10. 12
11. critical
12. 16
13. moody
14. no
15. forgetful
16. critical
17. moody
18. no
19. yes
20. ⎫
21. ⎪
22. ⎬ These will vary
23. ⎪
24. ⎪
25. ⎭

26. ⎫
27. ⎪
28. ⎬ These will vary
29. ⎪
30. ⎭
31.
32.
33.
34.
35.
36.
37.
38.
39.
40.
41.
42.
43.
44.
45.
46.
47.
48.
49.
50.

© 1983 by Dale Seymour Publications